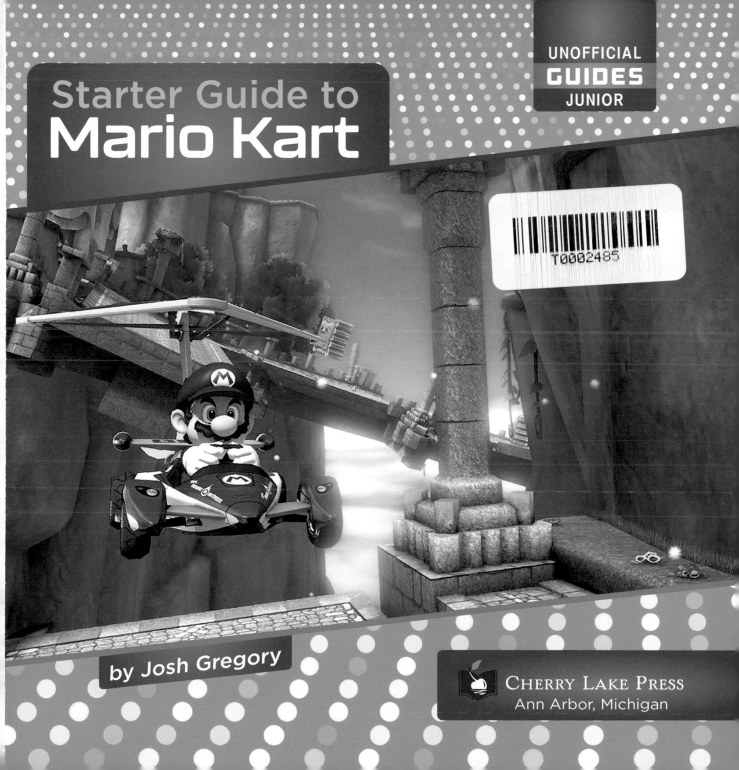

UNOFFICIAL
GUIDES
JUNIOR

Starter Guide to
Mario Kart

by Josh Gregory

CHERRY LAKE PRESS
Ann Arbor, Michigan

Published in the United States of America by Cherry Lake Publishing
Ann Arbor, Michigan
www.cherrylakepublishing.com

Reading Adviser: Beth Walker Gambro, MS, Ed., Reading Consultant, Yorkville, IL

Photo Credits: Images by Josh Gregory

Cherry Lake Press is an imprint of Cherry Lake Publishing Group.

Library of Congress Cataloging-in-Publication Data has been filed and is available at catalog.loc.gov

Printed in the United States of America by
Corporate Graphics

Note from the Publisher: Websites change regularly, and their future contents are outside of our control. Supervise children when conducting any recommended online searches for extended learning opportunities.

Contents

Let's Race!

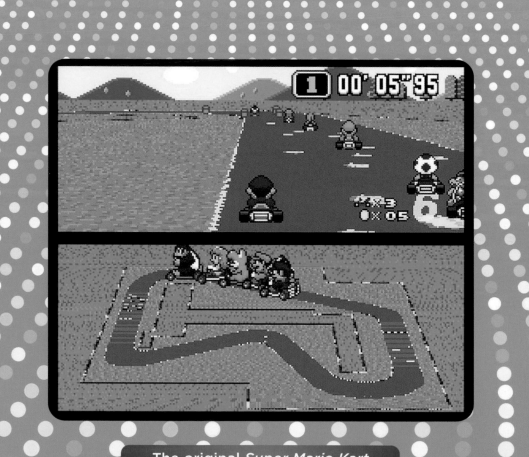

The original *Super Mario Kart* game had very simple **graphics**.

Ready, get set, go! The first *Super Mario Kart* game came out in 1992. It used characters from Nintendo's *Super Mario* series. Today, there are many games in the series. They include many more characters. Each game is a fun, action-packed adventure. Are you ready to race?

Rules of the Game

There are many characters to choose from in *Mario Kart*. Some characters are even from other video games!

Just about anyone can play *Mario Kart*. The **concept** is simple. Players **compete** in go-kart races. The goal is to reach the finish line first. But the game isn't easy or boring. There are many skills to learn. If you practice, you can become an expert!

The Starting Line

Speed
Acceleration
Weight
Handling
Traction

Paraglider

On a Nintendo Switch, if you press the + button while choosing your kart, you can turn on automatic steering by pressing L. Press R for automatic movement.

One of the most popular games is *Mario Kart 8*. It has 48 racecourses to choose from! Some look like real racetracks. Others look like amusement park rides. To **excel** at the game, you'll need to learn each one. Even the simplest course has surprises. For example, there are hidden shortcuts and **obstacles**.

Lots of Courses

Mario Kart 8 includes lots of new courses. You might find yourself driving through a world made of candy. Another course looks like a spooky mansion. There are classic courses too.

Game Modes

150 CONGRATULATIONS!

1	Waluigi	52
2	Baby Daisy	48
3	Luigi	43
4	Link	36
5	Toadette	29
6	Donkey Kong	26
7	Wendy	22
8	Shy Guy	20
9	Rosalina	16
10	Lemmy	15
10	Dry Bowser	15
12	Baby Rosalina	6

Earning trophies is one of the main goals in *Mario Kart 8*.

Each course can be played in different modes. The first is called Grand Prix. In this mode, you will choose among 12 events, or cups. Each cup is made up of four races. Players will earn points based on where they finish. Whoever finishes first gets the most points. After the four races, the player with the highest score wins.

Earning Trophies

You don't have to win every race in a cup to earn a first-place trophy. You just have to earn the most points.

Time Trials
and Ghosts

You can't attack a Ghost. You simply have to drive better to win!

In Time Trials mode, the goal is to finish as fast as you can. There are no other races. That's because you're racing against yourself! If you have a great race, you can save a Ghost. It's a recording of your race. Then you can race against the Ghost. You can also use your Ghost to challenge other players.

Battle Mode

You can attack other players as you race. This helps you move ahead. Some players prefer battling to racing. Then you don't have to worry about the finish line!

Multiplayer Action

If you are playing with friends, the screen will be split into sections for each player.

For many players, the real fun is competing with others. Choose "Multiplayer" from the main menu. Up to four players can join in the fun. Any other racers will be computer-controlled. You can pick Grand Prix or VS Race mode. You can also play online. Be careful. You might match up with the world's best players!

So Many Choices

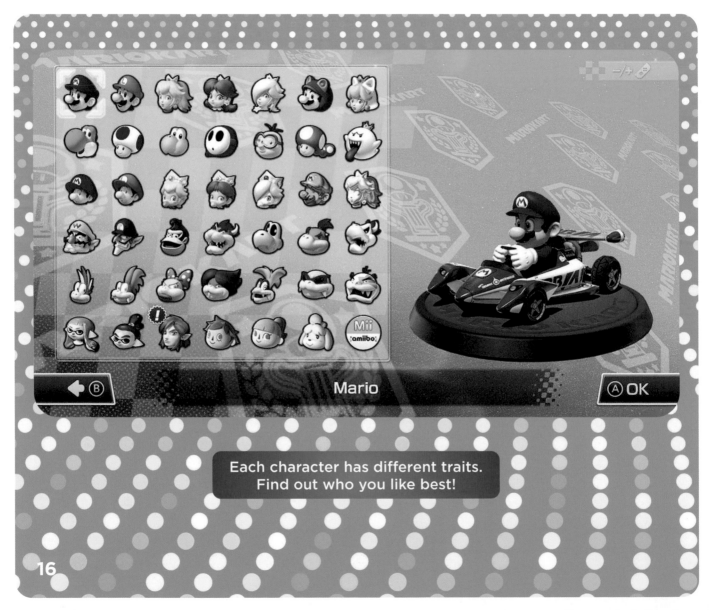

Mario

← B

Ⓐ OK

Each character has different traits.
Find out who you like best!

After you pick a mode, you need a character and a vehicle. There are lots of characters to choose from. Each one has different strengths. Try them out to see which ones you like. You can win with any of them. Now, it's time for a vehicle. There are many types. Some are really fast. Others are easier to steer. The choice is yours!

More to Explore

Players can jump and perform other stunts in the game!

There's more to learn once your race begins. You may find a question mark box. Each contains a special item. It could be a red turtle shell. You can use it to **sabotage** another player. A mushroom will give you speed. You'll also see coins on the track. Collect as many as you can. Every coin increases your speed. If you get hit or fall off the track, you'll lose your coins.

Drifting

Drifting is an important skill in *Mario Kart*. It allows you to make tight turns at high speeds. You know you're drifting when sparks fly!

What's Next?

Practice makes perfect. The more you play, the better racer you'll be!

Mastering *Mario Kart* takes plenty of practice! The best players don't win every time. But this is all part of the game. Remember that playing isn't just to win. It's to have fun! Laugh off mistakes and bad luck. There's always another race ahead of you!

GLOSSARY

compete (kuhm-PEET) to play against others in order to win

concept (KON-sept) a general idea

drifting (DRIF-ting) a way of turning a car that involves locking the tires and making them slide along the ground

excel (ek-SEL) to perform very well

graphics (GRAF-iks) images made by a computer

obstacles (OB-stuh-kulz) things that block a path or slow down progress

sabotage (SAB-uh-tahj) intentionally ruining someone's ability to do something